CELEBRATING OUR HOLIDAYS

Frederick Englund

Rosen Readers

Rosen Classroom™

New York

Published in 2013 by The Rosen Publishing Group, Inc.
29 East 21st Street, New York, NY 10010

Book Design: Michael Harmon

Photo Credits: Cover Comstock/Comstock Image/Getty Images; p. 4 moodboard/the Agency Collection/Getty Images; p. 5 Jamie Grill/Iconica/Getty Images; p. 6 Michael Kleih Photography/Flickr/Getty Images; p. 7 mistydawnphoto/Shutterstock.com; p. 8 Vsevolod33/Shutterstock.com; p. 9 Thinkstock Images/Comstock Images/Getty Images; pp. 10, 12 Ariel Skelley/Photographer's Choice/Getty Images; p. 11 Greg Adams Photography/Flickr/Getty Images; p. 13 Lisa Peardon/Digital Vision/Getty Images; p. 14 Jeff Cadge/The Image Bank/Getty Images; p. 16 (map) C. Sherburne/Photolink/Photodisc/Getty Images.

ISBN: 978-1-4488-8743-9
6-pack ISBN: 978-1-4488-8744-6

Manufactured in the United States of America

CPSIA Compliance Information: Batch #WS12RC: For further information contact Rosen Publishing, New York, New York at 1-800-237-9932.

Word Count: 132

CONTENTS

We live in the United States.
We have many U.S. holidays.

Can you think of any U.S. holidays?
How do you celebrate them?

Presidents' Day is in February.
What do we do on Presidents' Day?

We honor U.S. presidents
on Presidents' Day.

Memorial Day is in May.
What do we do on Memorial Day?

We honor U.S. soldiers on Memorial Day.
They keep us safe.

Independence Day is in July.
What do we do on Independence Day?

We honor our nation's birthday
on Independence Day.
We're glad to be free.

Thanksgiving is in November.
What do we do on Thanksgiving?

We give thanks for our family and friends on Thanksgiving.
We eat a special meal.

There are many U.S. holidays.
Can you think of any more?
What holiday do you like best?

WHEN ARE THE HOLIDAYS?

PRESIDENTS' DAY →	FEBRUARY
MEMORIAL DAY →	MAY
INDEPENDENCE DAY →	JULY
THANKSGIVING →	NOVEMBER

WORDS TO KNOW

soldiers

United States

INDEX